GUIDE TO
IRELAND

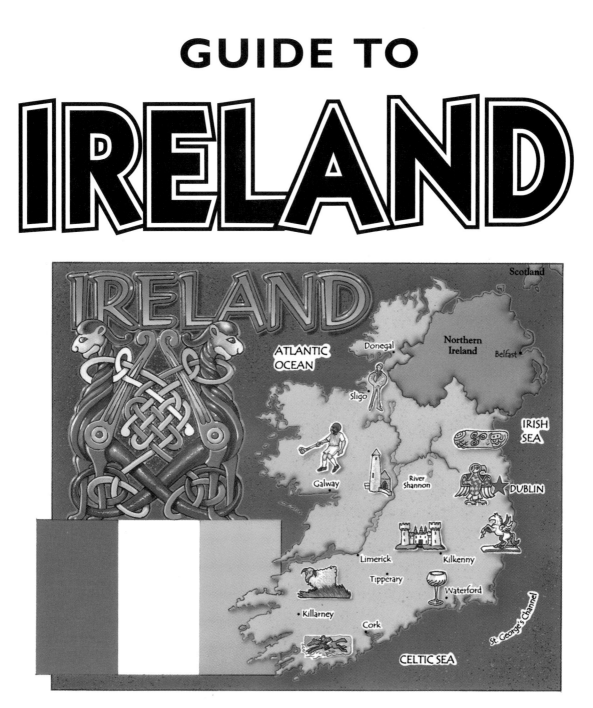

MICHAEL MARCH

Consultants: Valerie Coghlan and Geraldine O'Connor

Highlights for Children

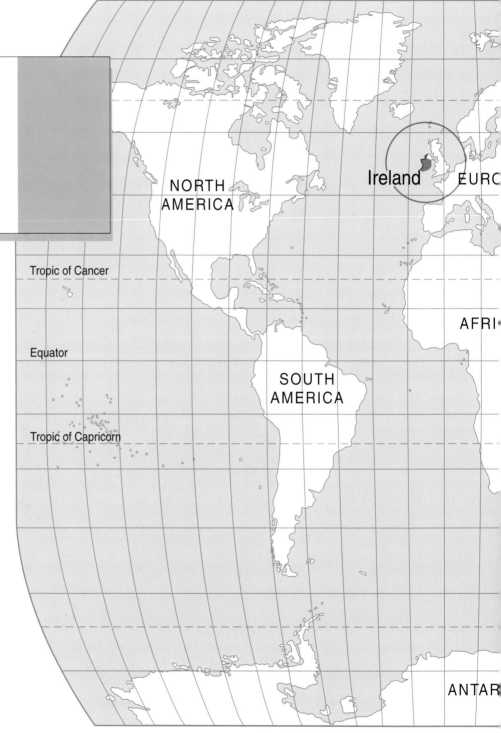

△ **Republic of Ireland flag** The design was introduced in 1848. It is based on the three colored bands of the French flag, the tricolor. Green represents the native people of Ireland (most of whom are Roman Catholic). Orange represents the British supporters of William of Orange, who settled in Northern Ireland in the 17th century (most of whom are Protestants). White stands for a lasting peace between the two groups.

NORTH AMERICA

Ireland

EURO

Tropic of Cancer

Equator

SOUTH AMERICA

Tropic of Capricorn

AFRI

ANTAR

ASIA

AUSTRALIA

CONTENTS

On the cover: Lackagh Bridge, on the Lackagh River in County Donegal, was built in the mid-eighteenth century. The river is famous for its salmon and trout fishing.

The publisher is grateful for the help of Valerie Coghlan, librarian at the Church of Ireland College of Education, Dublin. She is review editor of *Inis: The Children's Books Ireland Magazine.* She is also vice president of the Irish section of the International Board on Books for Young People (IBBY). The publisher also wishes to thank Geraldine O'Connor, a lecturer in social, environmental, and scientific education at the Church of Ireland College of Education. She is also an education officer for the Irish National Council for Curriculum and Assessment (NCCA) and a member of the Irish Association for Social, Scientific and Environmental Education (IASSEE).

Published by Highlights for Children
© 2003 Highlights for Children, Inc.
P.O. Box 18201
Columbus, Ohio 43218-0201
For information on *Top Secret Adventures,* visit www.tsadventures.com or call 1-800-962-3661.

10 9 8 7 6 5 4   HPS
ISBN 0-87534-576-X

REPUBLIC OF IRELAND AT A GLANCE

Area 27,136 square miles (70,553 square kilometers)

Population 4,156,119

Capital Dublin, population (including suburbs) 1,018,500

Other big cities Cork (119,418), Galway (72,414), Limerick (52,539)

Highest mountain Carrauntoohill, 3,414 feet (1,041 meters)

Longest river River Shannon, 230 miles (368 kilometers)

Largest lake Lough Corrib, 70 square miles (182 square kilometers)

Official languages Irish and English

▽ **Irish stamps** These depict the country's cultural history, countryside, and love of sports.

◁ **Irish money** The currency of the Republic of Ireland is the euro (€). The republic belongs to the European Union (EU) and has the same currency as other EU member countries. For example, this 10-euro note could be used in France or Germany.

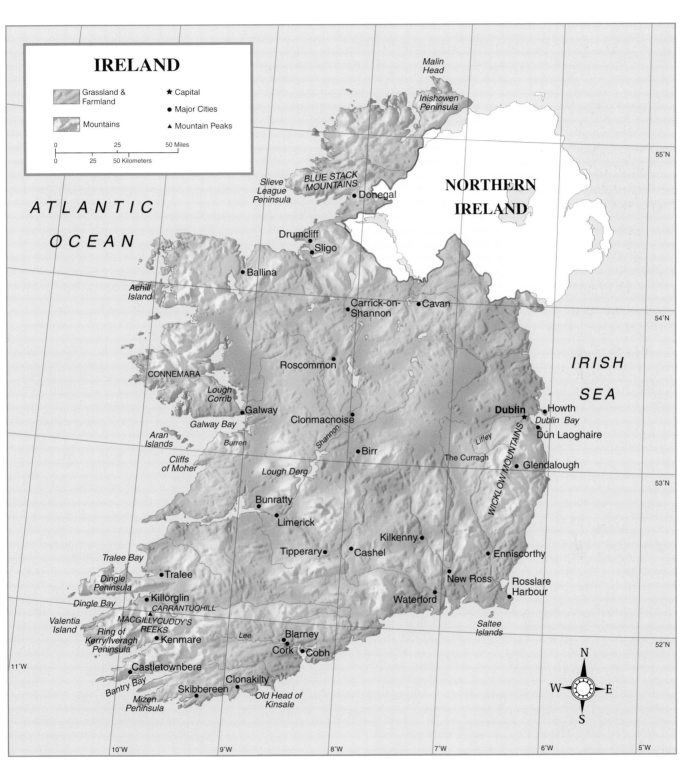

IRELAND

Grassland & Farmland

Mountains

★ Capital
● Major Cities
▲ Mountain Peaks

0   25   50 Miles
0   25   50 Kilometers

ATLANTIC

OCEAN

NORTHERN
IRELAND

IRISH

SEA

Malin
Head

Inishowen
Peninsula

Slieve
League
Peninsula

BLUE STACK
MOUNTAINS

● Donegal

Drumcliff
● Sligo

● Ballina

Achill
Island

Carrick-on-
Shannon

● Cavan

CONNEMARA

Lough
Corrib

● Galway

Galway Bay

Aran
Islands

Burren

Cliffs
of Moher

Roscommon

Clonmacnoise ●

Shannon

● Birr

Lough Derg

Bunratty ●

● Limerick

Tralee Bay

Dingle
Peninsula

● Tralee

Dingle Bay

● Killorglin

CARRANTUOHILL

Valentia
Island

MACGILLYCUDDY'S
REEKS

Ring of
Kerry/Iveragh
Peninsula

● Kenmare

Lee

Tipperary ●

● Cashel

Kilkenny ●

Blarney
●

Cork
●

● Cobh

11°W

Castletownbere ●

Bantry Bay

Skibbereen
●

Mizen
Peninsula

Clonakilty
●

Old Head of
Kinsale

Dublin ★

Howth
●

Dublin Bay

Dún Laoghaire

Liffey

The Curragh

WICKLOW MOUNTAINS

● Glendalough

● Enniscorthy

New Ross
●

Rosslare
Harbour

Waterford ●

Saltee
Islands

N
W   E
S

55°N

54°N

53°N

52°N

10°W   9°W   8°W   7°W   6°W   5°W

5

THE EMERALD ISLE

Ireland is an island in northwestern Europe. It is a bit larger than the state of West Virginia. To the north, west, and south, it is surrounded by the North Atlantic Ocean. On the east coast, the Irish Sea separates Ireland from Great Britain.

Ireland is known as The Emerald Isle because of the beautiful greenery of its landscapes. A ring of low mountains near the coasts rises above a central plain. Long, slow-moving rivers wind their way across the plain between lakes (or *loughs*) and wet ground, called bog.

Average daytime temperatures are 68 degrees F (20 degrees C) in summer and 45 degrees F (7.2 degrees C) in winter, so you won't be too hot or too cold in Ireland. But you may get wet. Snow is rare, but rain falls year-round, mostly in the west. The southeast corner of the country has the most sunshine.

The northeast corner of the island is called Northern Ireland and is part of the United Kingdom, or U.K. The U.K. also includes Great Britain, which is made up of England, Scotland, and Wales. You will be touring the Republic of Ireland, or Éire,

Ireland's Gaelic name, which includes 26 of the 32 Irish counties. The Republic of Ireland is an independent country of some 4.1 million people.

Many of the people you meet will be descendants of the Celts, who came here from mainland Europe thousands of years ago. The Irish have their own culture and rich tradition, which includes music, dancing, and sports. The native language is Irish, which is spoken in areas of the

▷ **Rainbow over Connemara** Sheep graze rough pasture on the hillslopes of the beautiful wilderness region of Connemara, in County Galway, western Ireland.

▷ **Irish musicians** In village halls and inns, people get together to enjoy the music, to converse, to sing and dance, and to eat and drink. Having a good time is what the Irish call *craic*.

country called the *Gaeltacht*. English is mostly spoken in the rest of the country. But the use of Irish is increasingly popular among the young.

As you travel the country by highway or railroad, you will see ancient buildings, some lively, modern cities, sheep and cattle pastures, and dramatic scenery. You will encounter the famous Irish hospitality and enjoy the exciting traditional music and dance for which Ireland is known worldwide.

▽ **St. Patrick's Day** Every year on March 17, Irish people take to town and city streets to celebrate their patron saint, St. Patrick. In the Republic of Ireland, St. Patrick's Day is a national holiday.

CITY ON THE LIFFEY

The republic's capital city, Dublin, stands on the banks of the River Liffey, near Dublin Bay on Ireland's east coast. Dublin was once an important Norse settlement. Viking weapons, tools, and jewelry found in Viking graves can be seen in the city's National Museum and Library. The name *Dublin* comes from the Irish *Dubh Linn*, which means "black pool."

If you join the crowds walking up the main thoroughfare, O'Connell Street, past cinemas, fashionable stores, cafés, and restaurants, you will come to the General Post Office building. In 1916, this was the center of a rebellion against British rule. Some bullet holes from the fighting can still be seen in the walls. The leaders of the uprising were imprisoned in Dublin's Kilmainham Gaol, which is now a museum. There, you can inspect the cells where they were held and see the courtyard where some of them were later executed by firing squad.

Trinity College, on the south bank of the Liffey, is Ireland's oldest university. It was founded in 1592 and has a distinctive domed, arched entranceway. The university library houses the *Book of Kells,* a beautiful illuminated manuscript of the Gospels

▽ **Trinity College Library** The old library building holds treasures such as the *Book of Durrow*, Ireland's oldest manuscript, and the *Book of Kells*.

created by monks in the nearby monastery of Kells more than 1,200 years ago.

Not far from Trinity College, you can visit Ireland's National Museum and Library and see Leinster House, where the Irish government meets. This fine old building was once the private home of a duke.

Walk on for a few blocks to Grafton Street, a wide shopping boulevard. Here, you can buy the latest fashions, as well as Irish pottery or other traditional souvenirs. Many nearby restaurants and cafés serve a wide variety of food, including pizza, hamburgers, ice cream, and the famous Irish stew.

△ **A hurler** Hurling is Ireland's oldest sport. Players use a hurley—a curved stick—to strike a ball and score goals and points against the opposing team. The All-Ireland finals take place in Dublin's Croke Park stadium.

◁ **Four Courts, Dublin** The impressive building, on the north bank of the Liffey, is the seat of the highest court in the Republic of Ireland. It was completed in 1802 but was damaged in 1922 when civil war broke out.

SUBURBS AND BEYOND

An electric rail service runs between downtown Dublin and the city's suburbs on the coast. The railroad is called DART (Dublin Area Rapid Transit).

If you take the northbound DART to the end of the line, you arrive in Howth. This pretty town sits on the edge of a rugged peninsula. In Howth Harbor, you will see fishing boats and private yachts moored along the quayside.

The DART heading south skirts Dublin Bay, where the River Liffey meets the Irish Sea. Here in the city's docklands, ferries carry foot passengers, cars, and trucks to and from Great Britain and France.

Traveling farther down the line, past the port of Dún Laoghaire, you come to Sandycove. You can visit a stone tower that has been turned into a museum in memory of James Joyce, author of *Ulysses* and one of Ireland's greatest writers.

Inland, to the south, the Wicklow Mountains rise to more than 2,000 feet (610 meters). Here, the ancient ruins of Glendalough monastery nestle in a deep

▽ **Heather on the Wicklow Mountains** The high Wicklow peaks can be seen from Dublin Bay. The mountains offer spectacular views of waterfalls, lakes, valleys, and deep gorges.

△ **The Glendalough monastery ruins** The 100-foot-high (30-meter) round tower was built in the tenth century. It served as a watchtower and rest place for the monks.

valley beside two lakes. The monastery was begun in the A.D. 500s by a Christian monk named Kevin, who was later made a saint. The site also includes the remains of churches and other buildings that were added in the centuries that followed.

Ireland's oldest hiking trail passes Glendalough. About 20 miles (32 kilometers) back down the trail, Powerscourt Waterfall, often swollen by rain, makes a spectacular drop of nearly 400 feet (122 meters).

△ **Powerscourt Gardens, County Wicklow** The terraced gardens on the Powerscourt estate include roses, conifers, eucalyptus, and beech trees. The gardens were created in the eighteenth century and redesigned a hundred years later to look the way they do today.

11

HORSES, HISTORY, AND LEGEND

Ireland is famous for its horses. The Curragh, in County Kildare, consists of 5,000 acres (2,000 hectares) of green turf, where Thoroughbreds graze and train for the races. Horse racing here goes back more than 2,000 years. Today, the Irish Derby, run every summer at The Curragh racecourse, is one of the world's major horse-racing events.

▽ **Stone Age burial site** The Newgrange Megalithic Passage Tomb in County Meath was built so that once a year in December—the day of the Winter Solstice—sunshine could enter the burial chamber through the roof box.

The River Boyne begins its course in the bog of County Kildare and flows northeast into the thickly wooded Boyne Valley. Here, in 1690, King William III, a Protestant, defeated King James II, a Roman Catholic, in a battle for the throne of England. William's victory was a bitter blow for Irish Catholics, and it has shaped the course of Ireland's history till the present day.

On the south-facing slope of the valley, you can explore ancient burial sites that are more than 4,000 years old. The people of that time used huge stones, which they may have brought from the Wicklow Mountains, to build underground burial chambers connected by tunnels.

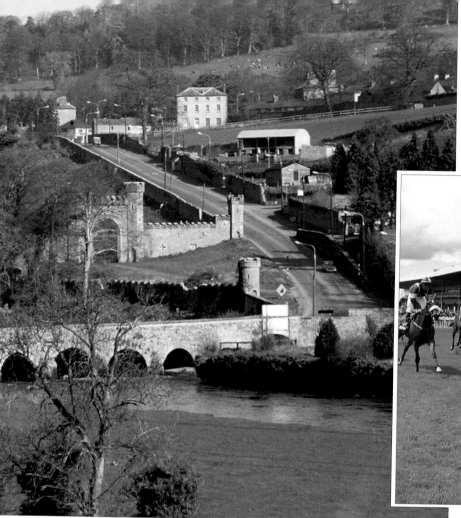

◁ **Slane Bridge over the River Boyne** The road from the river leads to Slane Castle, which is known for its many concerts.

△ **Derby Day at The Curragh** The Irish Derby is one of the country's major sporting and social events. Every summer, three-year-old Thoroughbreds run the 1 1/2-mile (2.4-kilometer) race, competing for big prizes for their owners and a place in the record books.

The Hill of Tara, to the southwest of Newgrange, features in many ancient Irish legends. Today, Tara is important because it has one of the largest lead and zinc mines in Europe.

In neighboring County Offaly, you can take a ride on a narrow-gauge railroad through the Blackwater Bog and try your hand at cutting peat. Bog is land that is spongy and wet year-round. Peat is a dark brown, compact material that is formed in the bog by vegetation that decays over thousands of years. For centuries, Irish people have burned peat as fuel in the home. Today, much of the peat is harvested by machine. It is burned in power stations to generate electricity.

TO THE LAND OF YEATS

Roscommon is an old market town deep in the middle of sheep and cattle country northwest of Dublin. Outside the town, on a hillside, lie the ruins of a once-great castle. It was built by the Normans in the 1200s. The Normans, from France, had conquered England in the 1000s and entered Ireland soon after. Roscommon Castle then passed through many different hands until the late 1600s, when the English captured and destroyed it.

To the north of Roscommon are the lush, green hills of County Leitrim. Here, in Carrick-on-Shannon, you can fish for pike in Ireland's longest river, the Shannon. The town marks the most northerly point of the river that is navigable by boats.

Beyond the Shannon lies Sligo, the most northerly commercial port on Ireland's west coast. In old Sligo town, the narrow, one-way downtown streets fill with traffic during the day. Sligo docks echo with the noises of ships loading and unloading their cargoes.

West of the town, Knocknarea Mountain rises above the long sand dunes that fringe Sligo Bay. Windsurfing is popular here, but swimming is dangerous. A famous grave can be seen at Drumcliff, on the route north to Donegal. The great Irish poet William Butler Yeats, who died in France in 1939, is buried there. Donegal town was once the stronghold of the Irish O'Donnell family, who controlled the region for 400 years. You can visit their castle, which for a long time was in ruins but has now been restored. In the town, you can buy the cloth famously known as Donegal tweed and watch it being woven on handlooms.

◁ **Statue of W. B. Yeats** The poet Yeats was born in Dublin but was inspired by the landscapes of County Sligo, where he is buried. In 1923, he was awarded the Nobel Prize for literature.

▷ **Fishmonger with Irish salmon** Around 200,000 salmon, totaling some 600 tons (600 tonnes), are landed each year. Most of them are caught offshore in drift nets. Salmon fishing on the River Shannon is popular with anglers.

▽ **Sligo Harbor** This busy port handles bulk cargoes of timber, fish meal, steel, fertilizer, grain, and peat.

THE FAR NORTH

County Donegal is a beautiful highland wilderness, with a rugged coastline that is battered by Atlantic gales in winter. No trains come here, and buses between the county's smaller towns run only once a day. When Ireland was ruled by the English, this was one of the last regions to fall under their control. Still today, Irish traditions are stronger here. Many Irish-speaking areas are found in County Donegal.

The highway going west from Donegal town to the coast climbs sharply to more than 1,000 feet (305 meters). From high up, you can view the sheer cliffs and the sea below. The eastbound route from the coast goes through the steep Glengesh Pass, twisting its way round hairpin bends to the river at the bottom.

Farther north, you can visit Glenveagh National Park, where one of the largest herds of red deer in Europe roams the bogs, mountain glens, and forests of oak and birch.

On the north coast, the winter storms can be so fierce that, in the past, villagers tied down the thatched roofs on their cottages with rope. Most houses now have slate or tiled roofs. Malin Head, a tiny fishing village at the tip of the rocky Inishowen Peninsula, is the northernmost point in all Ireland.

From Donegal town, you change buses at Ballina to reach Westport, near the west coast of County Mayo. Westport is an elegant town built in the late 1700s. Westport's huge mansion, Westport House, was built on the spot where, some 150 years earlier, the castle of the pirate queen Grace O'Malley had stood. You can still see the remains of the dungeons.

▷ **Winter in the Donegal highlands** The center of County Donegal is made up of mountains crossed by narrow, winding glens.

▷ Lough Veagh in Glenveagh National Park
The picturesque lake is well known for its trout and salmon fishing.

▽ Grianán of Aileach, County Donegal The circular stone fort, built on a hilltop, is a reconstruction of one that stood here more than 1,000 years ago. This was once the stronghold of the mighty O'Neill clan.

GOING SOUTH

Lough Corrib, in County Galway, is the largest lake in the Republic of Ireland. A wild landscape of mountains, bog, and small lakes and streams stretches from the western shores of Lough Corrib to the sandy coast dotted with islands. This region is called Connemara. Here, you will find Irish-speaking people. The region is famous for its dry-stone walls and the Connemara pony, a small, hardy horse.

Galway town was founded by the Anglo-Normans more than 800 years ago. Today, it is the largest town in western Ireland. It has two universities, modern industries such as electronics, and many theaters. The oldest part of town is called the Claddagh, which gave its name to the Claddagh ring. Claddagh rings have been made here for hundreds of years and are still popular all over Ireland. Oysters caught in Galway Bay, when in season, are the local delicacy. They are celebrated in a festival held in September.

▷ **Cliffs of Moher** One of Ireland's most famous sights, the Cliffs of Moher attract busloads of tourists as well as thousands of seabirds, which make their home in the cliffs.

▽ **Poulnabrone Dolmen** The 6,000-year-old tomb, on the Burren's limestone pavements, is built of vertical stones with a huge capstone on top. It is one of the finest examples of a portal tomb, or dolmen, in Ireland.

Ferries cross Galway Bay west to the nearby Aran Islands. On Inishmore, the largest of the three islands, you can explore Dún Aengus, a clifftop, ring-shaped fort built during the Iron Age. Walls 18 feet (5 meters) thick form a semicircle around the cliff edge high above the ocean. While on the island, you can shop for an Aran sweater—the heavy, hand-knitted, woolen pullover for which the islands are famous.

On a clear day, you can see the Aran Islands from the Cliffs of Moher, in County Clare, to the south. These spectacular, dark sandstone cliffs stretch along the coast for nearly 5 miles (8 kilometers) and drop sheer into the Atlantic Ocean from a height of more than 600 feet (183 meters).

A huge limestone plateau covers much of County Clare. It is called the Burren and is a vast expanse of white, almost completely barren stone, looking like the surface of the moon. There is some life on the Burren, however. Wildflowers that are found nowhere else in Ireland grow here. In some places, the limestone is cracked, which has caused rivers to flow underground and caves to form.

◁ **On board the ferry to the Aran Islands** An Irish-speaking region, the islands are a popular tourist destination. Inishmore, the biggest island, is about 8 miles (13 kilometers) long and has 900 or so inhabitants.

OLD BUILDINGS AND MUSEUMS

A tall castle with square turrets stands on the banks of the Bunratty River, on the edge of County Clare on Ireland's west coast. The castle has been restored to look the way it did in the 1400s. The brave can admire a wonderful view from the battlements. In the evening in the castle's Great Hall, you can sit down to a medieval feast presented by women wearing medieval costumes.

More buildings dating from the Middle Ages can be seen in the city of Limerick. In 1168, Dónall Mór O'Brien, an Irish king, founded St. Mary's Cathedral here. So keen was he to build the church that he used parts of his own palace in the construction. Inside, you can admire beautiful wall carvings depicting the struggle between good and evil.

Today, Limerick, which is located on the wide estuary of the River Shannon, is an important industrial city. Bacon curing and grain milling started here in the 1800s. More recently, factories producing computers and electronic components have sprung up. You will also find traditional crafts, such as lace making. The lace is made using decorative stitches to create Celtic patterns. Nearby is Shannon Airport, the most westerly airfield in Europe.

Tralee is the main town of County Kerry. There, you can visit a museum showing the history of the region from 8000 B.C. to the present. "The Rose of Tralee" is a well-known Irish song. Every summer, the town holds a festival in which young women of Irish descent come from far and wide to compete for the Rose of Tralee title.

Just outside Tralee, at Blennerville, you can see Ireland's largest working windmill. Blennerville once was Kerry's biggest port of emigration. In the 1840s, many thousands of Irish people sailed to the United States of America to escape famine when their potato crops failed. A small museum here tells their story.

▽ **King John's Castle, Limerick city** The castle was built by the Normans on the east bank of the River Shannon in the early 1200s. In the castle courtyard, you can see replicas of medieval battering rams.

National Folk Theatre, Tralee
Performances include dance, music, and mime that capture the traditions of Irish rural life. The Irish name for the troupe is *Siamsa Tíre*.

Adare town, County Limerick
The pretty town's main street is lined with 200-year-old thatched-roof cottages. Other buildings, such as the ruined castle, are much older.

SOUTHWESTERN PENINSULAS

Long, ragged-shaped peninsulas jut out into the sea between deep bays on Ireland's southwest coast. Slea Head, at the tip of Dingle Peninsula, is the site of some 400 beehive-shaped houses, or *clocháns*. They were built in early Christian times, using overlapping tiers of stones to hold the structure together. In those days, builders had no mortar to hold stones in place.

You will find more beehive houses south of Dingle Bay, on the Iveragh Peninsula. Here, too, you can travel the famous Ring of Kerry. This is the popular name for the route that loops round the Iveragh coast, offering fine views all the way. You pass pretty villages, ancient ruins, and mountains and lakes on the 112-mile (179-kilometer) journey.

You also pass the town of Killarney, by Lough Leane. On the opposite side of the lake are mountains called Macgillycuddy's Reeks. They include Mount Carrauntoohill, the highest peak in Ireland. Lough Leane is part of Killarney National Park, an area of great natural beauty. To tour the park, you can hire a traditional horse-drawn cart (jaunting car) and driver.

▷ **Reask stone on the Dingle Peninsula**
The stone pillar, decorated with a cross and old Latin inscriptions, stands amid the ruins of a monastery. It is an important early Celtic Christian monument.

△ **Slea Head** Rough stone walls cut across the hills that top the jagged cliffs of Slea Head. This dramatic scenery was the setting for the film *Far and Away.*

On the north coast of Beara Peninsula are abandoned copper mines. The mountains near Allihies village are dotted with deserted cottages and fenced-off mine shafts. This was once a prosperous mining community, but mining has long since ceased here. On the peninsula's south coast, the little town of Castletownbere is one of Ireland's major fishing ports.

Mizen Head is the southwest tip of Ireland. From here, you can cross a bridge, suspended 150 feet (46 meters) above the sea, to an old lighthouse building. The building is now a museum, showing the work of lightkeepers as well as information on shipwrecks and local marine life, such as dolphins, seals, and whales.

△ **Little Skellig** The rocky outcrop called Little Skellig juts out of the sea off the coast of the Iveragh Peninsula. The rock and its companion, Skellig Michael, are home to nesting gannets.

23

Triumphs and Tragedies

Every July, the little town of Clonakilty in the southern county of Cork celebrates the Black and White Pudding Festival. Black pudding was invented here in the 1800s at a time of food shortages. It includes scraps of pig meat and looks like a large sausage. White pudding is similar but also contains milk. Fried slices of black or white pudding are part of a traditional Irish breakfast.

▽ **Cobh** The town of Cobh was once a transatlantic port and a health resort. In the nineteenth century it was renamed Queenstown, after Britain's Queen Victoria, but the name was changed back to Cobh when the Republic of Ireland gained its independence.

At Woodfield, just outside Clonakilty, you can see a memorial bust of the Irish patriot Michael Collins. He was born here in 1890 and became one of the leaders of Ireland's struggle for independence against British rule. He also died not far from here, at Béal na mBláth, when he was ambushed in 1922 during the Irish Civil War.

With a population around 120,000, Cork is the Republic of Ireland's second-largest city after Dublin. It was founded by St. Fin Barre, who built a monastery here by the banks of the River Lee, in the 600s. You can visit St. Fin Barre's Cathedral, which, it is said, stands on the same site. This beautiful limestone church with three tall spires was built in the 1800s.

Blarney is only a short bicycle ride from Cork. Here, you can explore a castle in which you will find the famous Blarney Stone. It is said that if you kiss the Blarney Stone, you will gain the gift of being a good talker. To reach the stone, you have to lie down, stretching your head backward.

Cobh (pronounced "cove"), by Cork Harbor, was once a major seaport. Until the 1960s, many Irish emigrating to the United States of America and Canada would set sail from here. This was also the last port of call for the famous passenger liner *Titanic*, which tragically sank in 1912. Today, Cobh is an important fishing port and one of Ireland's main yachting centers.

▷ **Kissing the Blarney Stone** To reach the stone to kiss it, you have to lie on your back and suspend your head over a hole in the castle wall. An attendant holds your legs to keep you steady.

▽ **The spires of St. Fin Barre's Cathedral** Over the centuries, 11 churches have been built on this site, including three cathedrals.

County Tipperary, in south central Ireland, is known for its coal mining, dairy cattle, and potato farms. It also has fascinating historical sites.

The Rock of Cashel rises about 200 feet (61 meters) above the Tipperary plain. Over 1,500 years ago, St. Patrick, the patron saint of Ireland, stood at the top to baptize the king of the southwestern province of Munster. Today, you will find here the ruins of churches built in the Middle Ages. The finest of these is Cormac's Chapel, with its distinctive twin towers.

Ireland's best-preserved medieval town is Kilkenny. Kilkenny Castle, on the banks of the River Nore, was built in the 1200s. The hallway is paved with marble dug from local quarries. Outside the town, you can explore the gigantic Dunmore Cave, known as "the darkest place in Ireland."

Trains from Dublin stop at Kilkenny on their way to Waterford town. Waterford is a big seaport, where cranes line the harbor, but it is most famous for its crystal glassware. The factory where this was first produced, in 1783, is a popular stop for tourists. Here, you can watch glassware being made, from the molding of the molten glass to the final polishing.

The ancient town of Wexford, on the southeast coast, is today a tourist center and a busy ferry terminal. North of here, you can visit Enniscorthy, which holds its Strawberry Festival every July. Eating locally grown strawberries, traditional dancing, and greyhound racing are all part of the colorful celebrations.

▷ **Waterford crystal** The sparkling crystal glassware produced by the master craftspeople at the Waterford factory is world famous and has brought prosperity to the town.

▷ **Kilkenny Castle** For more than 600 years the castle was the home of the earls of Ormonde, whose family name was Butler. In 1967, the castle was given to the people of Kilkenny.

If you climb Vinegar Hill, you will have a fine view over the town. In 1798, the people of Enniscorthy rebelled against British rule but were defeated by British troops at the Battle of Vinegar Hill. They rose up again in 1916 to support the uprising in Dublin. This brings you back to the point where your tour of the Republic of Ireland began.

◁ **Kilkenny town** Many of the town's buildings have been restored to look the way they did in the Middle Ages. Narrow alleyways, called slips, follow the pattern of medieval streets.

27

REPUBLIC OF IRELAND FACTS AND FIGURES

People

Most Irish people are descended from the ancient Celts of mainland Europe. Others have ancestors who were English or who came from Normandy in northern France. Recently, people from Africa, Asia, and other parts of Europe have settled in the Republic of Ireland. In the past, large numbers of Irish people went to live abroad. As a result, many United States, Canadian, British, and Australian citizens are of Irish descent.

Trade and Industry

Irish factories produce dairy products and processed foods and drinks in addition to computers, electronic equipment, chemicals, machinery, furniture, glassware, clothing, and other goods for sale abroad. The Irish Republic is a member of the European Union (EU), and most of its trade is with Great Britain as well as Germany, France, and other EU members. Some energy needs are provided by hydroelectric power from the Rivers Shannon, Erne, and Liffey.

△ **Sea angling, County Kerry** Throughout Ireland, fishing by rod and line from the shore is a trade, tourist attraction, and popular pastime.

Peat (also known as turf) is another local energy source. But most of the country's energy comes from oil, coal, and gas, much of which is imported.

Farming

Beef or dairy cattle are reared in the midlands, the south, the north, and the east. Sheep are kept for their wool and their meat and are found throughout the country. The main crops are barley, oats, potatoes, turnips, and sugar beets. Barley is used to make Irish whiskey and the dark-colored stout beers such as Guinness. These alcoholic drinks are important export products.

Fishing

Horse mackerel, mackerel, whiting, and herring make up most of the deep-sea catch. Sole, plaice, monkfish, turbot, and haddock account for much of the rest. Mussels, crabs, lobsters, crawfish, prawns, and oysters are caught near the coasts. Salmon and trout are fished in rivers, lakes, and mountain streams. Some fish are bred on fish farms in coastal bays or river mouths.

Food

Traditional dishes are usually simple to prepare and are boiled or fried.

Irish stew Mutton or lamb cooked with parsley and potatoes, onions, and other vegetables such as carrots, leeks, or cabbage

Irish breakfast Lightly fried bacon, sausages cooked till brown on both sides, fried eggs, fried tomatoes or mushrooms, and slices of fried black and white pudding

Boxty Fried potato cakes made with mashed potato, grated raw potato, eggs, milk, and flour and served with a tangy applesauce

Schools

Children must attend school between the ages of six and fifteen, although most children begin at age four and finish at seventeen or eighteen. Schooling is free of charge. All children learn Irish. In a growing number of schools, all subjects are taught in the Irish language. These schools are called *Gaelscoileanna.* After completing secondary school, many students go on to a university, a college, or an institute of technology.

Religion

There is no official religion in the Irish republic. Traditionally, most Irish people are Christians. The Roman Catholic Church has by far the greatest number of members. Some people belong to

△ **A tractor cutting hay on an Irish farm**
Farming has always been important to the Republic of Ireland. Meat, milk, and cheeses are among the country's leading exports.

the Church of Ireland (Episcopalian) and smaller Protestant church groups. In Ireland there are also members of other world religions, such as Islam, Judaism, Buddhism, and Hinduism.

The Media

The most popular daily newspapers published in the republic are the *Irish Times* and *Irish Independent,* both in English.

The *Irish Times* prints weekly columns in Irish. *Foinse* is an all-Irish-language weekly newspaper.

The Irish-language television channel TG4 attracts some 730,000 viewers every day. RTÉ, the national television and radio station, broadcasts most programs in English but also some in Irish. Viewers and listeners can also receive programs, transmitted by cable or satellite, in English, Irish, and foreign languages.

Literature and Drama

Ireland is a land of folklore, fables, and legends, such as the heroic exploits of *Finn McCool,* which were recorded in early poetry in the native Irish language. Since then, Irish writers, poets, and playwrights have achieved worldwide fame. They include Jonathan Swift (1667–1745), who wrote *Gulliver's Travels;* Oscar Wilde (1854–1900); George Bernard Shaw (1856–1950); the poet W. B. Yeats (1865–1939); James Joyce (1882–1941), author of *Ulysses;* and the playwright Samuel Beckett (1906–1989).

REPUBLIC OF IRELAND FACTS AND FIGURES

Visual Arts

More than 1,000 years ago, the Irish monasteries produced works of art in the form of illuminated manuscripts, such as the *Book of Kells.* From the 1700s to today, Irish painters, including members of the Hone family and Jack B. Yeats (brother of the poet W. B. Yeats), gained widespread recognition for their work.

Music and Dance

Traditional Irish music and dance go together. The music is played on fiddle, tin whistle, pipes, and *bodrhán* (hand-held drum). The dancing includes high kicks and stamping while keeping the back straight. Traditional music has influenced modern Irish performers such as Enya, U2, and The Corrs.

Holidays and Festivals

Christian holidays such as Easter are celebrated throughout the country. Here are a few of the other festivals that are enjoyed.

March 17 **St. Patrick's Day**
  A national holiday when people wear shamrocks and join in street parades to celebrate the

△ **A badger near the entrance to its lair**
Badgers are common in some woods in Ireland.

country's patron saint.

June 16 **Bloomsday** Dubliners act out scenes from James Joyce's novel *Ulysses,* which is about a day in the life of a fictional Dublin man named Leopold Bloom.

August 10–12 **Puck Fair** People of Killorglin, in County Kerry, have fun in a mock ceremony involving the crowning of a goat.

Mid-September **Oyster Festival** Street theater and oyster-opening contests are part of celebrations held in Galway town.

Sports

Gaelic football is a traditional game played between two teams of 15 players, a little like American football. Hurling is similar, but players use a curved stick to propel a smaller ball. Hurling is Ireland's oldest sport. Handball, another Irish game, resembles squash, except that hands are used instead of rackets. Soccer, boxing, golf, and horse racing are among the other sports that Irish people enjoy playing or watching.

Plants

Grasses, rushes, ferns, and sedges are the most common plants. Gorse and hawthorn grow on hillsides. On the Burren, in County Clare, alpine flowers are found alongside Mediterranean plants such as orchids.

Animals

Deer, badgers, squirrels, Irish stoats, Irish hares, bats, foxes, and mice inhabit the woodlands, bogs, and mountains. Lizards are also found, but no snakes. Otters and mink make their homes by the rivers and lakes. Gray seals and other species live along the coasts, and dolphins swim in inshore waters. Waterfowl and field birds are common.

HISTORY

People have lived in Ireland for 9,000 years. In about 500 B.C., the island was invaded by the Celts. In the A.D.100s came Roman traders, who called the country Hibernia. In the 400s, St. Patrick, who had been a slave, converted the people to Christianity. First the Vikings and then the Normans invaded the island in the centuries that followed.

In 1541, Henry VIII of England declared himself king of Ireland. Under the Tudors, English and Scottish people moved in and settled on the land. Roman Catholics were persecuted in an attempt to force Irish people to become Protestants. In 1801, England made Ireland part of the United Kingdom of Great Britain and Ireland. During the mid-1800s, disease destroyed the Irish potato crop. About a million Irish people died of starvation, and more fled abroad.

In 1916, Irish patriots in Dublin rose up against the British, but the rebellion was crushed. Three years later, an Irish parliament met in Dublin and declared Ireland an independent republic. Fierce fighting followed between Irish republicans and the British. Eventually, a treaty was forged, splitting Ireland in two. The Irish Free State, which included most of the island, was given partial independence, while Northern Ireland remained part of the United Kingdom.

Opponents of the treaty, who wanted independence for the whole of Ireland, were defeated in a civil war. In 1949, the Irish Free State—then called Éire—became the fully independent Republic of Ireland. The prime minister's title in Gaelic is *Taoiseach*.

LANGUAGE

The Irish language, called Irish Gaelic, stems from the language spoken by the Celts. It is related to Scottish Gaelic, another Celtic language. Irish and Scottish Gaelic developed as separate languages from about A.D. 900. The Republic of Ireland has two official languages: Irish and English. More Irish people speak English than speak Irish. The Irish-speaking areas are called the *Gaeltacht*. They are mostly in the west and northwest.

Useful words and phrases

English	Irish
one	*aon*
two	*dó*
three	*trí*
four	*ceathair*
five	*cúig*
six	*sé*
seven	*seacht*
eight	*ocht*
nine	*naoi*
ten	*deich*
Sunday	*Domhnach*
Monday	*Luan*
Tuesday	*Mháirt*

Useful words and phrases

English	Irish
Wednesday	*Chéadaoin*
Thursday	*Déardaoin*
Friday	*Aoine*
Saturday	*Satharn*
Good morning	*Dia duit ar maidin*
Hello	*Dia duit*
Good evening	*Tráthnóna maith duit*
Good night	*Oíche mhaith*
Good-bye	*Slán agat*
Please	*Más é do thoil é*
Thank you	*Go raibh míle maith agat*
How are you?	*Conas atá tú?*

INDEX

Acknowledgments
Book created for Highlights for Children, Inc., by Bender Richardson White.
Editor: Lionel Bender
Designer: Richard Johnson
Art Editor: Ben White
Picture Researcher: Cathy Stastny
Production: Kim Richardson

Map and flag produced by Stefan Chabluk.
Currency from MRI Bankers Guide to Foreign Currency.
Stamps courtesy of Scott Publishing Co., Sidney, OH 45365 (www.scottonline.com).

Editorial Consultant: Andrew Gutelle
Guide to Ireland was produced with the help of the Ireland Tourist Board, London
Ireland Consultants: Valerie Coghlan and Geraldine O'Connor
Editorial Coordinator, Highlights for Children: Joan Hyman

Picture credits
All photos are copyright Bord Fáilte Eireann—Irish Tourist Board except for pages 12, Eye Ubiquitous/Hugh Rooney; 14, James Davis Travel Photography; 30, Corbis Images/Pat Jerrold/Papilio.

Special thanks to Derek Cullen at Bord Fáilte Photography Library, Dublin, for supplying many of the images used in this book.

Illustration on page 1 by Tom Powers.